I WANNA
RE-DO MY ROOM

by

Clea Hantman

illustrated by
Azadeh Houshyar

ALADDIN PAPERBACKS
New York   London   Toronto   Sydney

ALADDIN PAPERBACKS

An imprint of Simon & Schuster Children's Publishing Division

1230 Avenue of the Americas, New York, NY 10020

Designed by Azadeh Houshyar

The text of this book was set in Providence and Bokka.

The illustrations were rendered in black pen and Photoshop.

Manufactured in the United States of America

First Aladdin Paperbacks edition June 2006

10 9 8 7 6 5 4 3 2 1

Library of Congress Cataloging-in-Publication Data

Hantman, Clea.

I wanna re-do my room / by Clea Hantman ; illustrated by
Azadeh Houshyar—1st ed.

p. cm.

ISBN-13: 978-0-689-87463-5

ISBN-10: 0-689-87463-4

1. Handicraft for girls—Juvenile literature. 2. Girls' bedrooms—Juvenile
literature. 3. Children's rooms—Juvenile literature. 4. Interior decoration—
Juvenile literature. I. Houshyar, Azadeh. II. Title.

TT171.H36 2006

745.5—dc22   2005006955

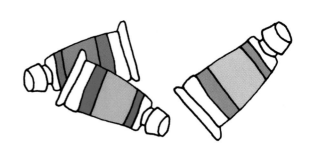

Clea's Dedication:
For all the girls aching to get out
of the box and into a new
stylish space. Rock on.

Azadeh's Dedication:
For Kermit, with love.

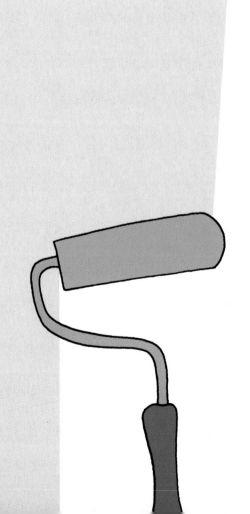

CONTENTS

the intro

. . . .

Is your room still full of artifacts from your toddler years? Do the goods surrounding you speak to your tastes . . . or your mom's? Look around. Your room should be a safe haven for you, it should be comfortable, it should be functional. It should also be all about you. Oh, and don't forget—it should be fun!

The best way to do this is to create a bunch of things with your very own two hands. Consider this book your most basic instructional how-to—your inspiration. And I hope you'll take these ideas and make them your very own. Soon enough your private space will be a showplace, a paean to your personality, four walls full of fun, an efficient, exciting extension of you.

xoxo clea

what you need
to make the projects in this book:

creativity

a love of all things
messy and dirty

boundless energy

a handful
of cheap supplies

What you don't need
to make the projects in this book:

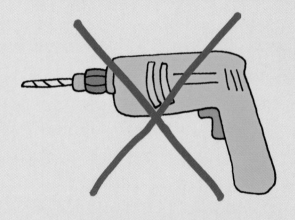

heavy machinery

CHAPTER ONE

hello, walls

· ·

You don't need a whole new set of furniture to make your room feel new. A little paint and a project or two, and your room can be transformed from simple to stunning, from boring to bodaciously beautiful! And while it takes a little more effort than going to the store and buying new stuff, it's thoroughly worth a little paint under your nails. But be forewarned: The projects that lie ahead call for you to don your junkiest clothes.

You already know how to paint. You learned in kindergarten. If your room seems large and daunting, enlist a friend or three to help. Treat them to caramel white chocolate mochas before you start.

Now, I could go long and hard into color theory, but I won't bore you. Actually, I know **nothing** about color theory, so you're totally safe. But I know what I like, and I bet you do too, once you see it. The wall of beautiful, multihued paint cards at the local hardware store is the perfect place to begin. Run your fingers over the plentiful pinks, the boodles of blues, and the gaggle of greens. Those colorful little cards are there to help. They are free. This isn't a license to scoop up every last one and cart them all home, but do pick up a few extras, as they make terrific note cards and great little pieces of mini artwork for your walls.

You needn't get fancy with paint treatments and faux-sueded walls. And the fad of sponge-painted walls ("But it looks like clouds!") is **so** over—save the sponges for the sink. But with just traditional paint techniques that you already know, you can create wildly cool and unique room décor. You've just got to know how to wield the tape! But more on that in a moment.

A Few Prepaint Pointers

This is going to sound so silly, but you may have to clean your walls before you paint. Paint doesn't like to stick to dirt. So make sure your walls are dirt-free. If you have any tiny holes in your wall, patch 'em up with this junk folks call "joint compound." It's pasty and goopy, like frosting on a cake. When it dries, you can sand it down with a piece of sandpaper and you're ready, set, go.

When buying paint, there are so many choices. Matte, flat, shiny, eggshell, glossy . . . And then there are the oil- and latex-based mixtures, and, well, it can get mighty confusing! Something with a little gloss (anything but matte or flat) is going to be easier to clean, but matte paint is pretty. It's your call. Latex is much preferred over anything else because paint is smelly enough without adding even more chemicals to the mix.

You'll need to pick up a roller and a roller cover (the fuzzy thing that goes on the roller). FYI: The roller cover is removable and comes in many different textures. Go for one that isn't very fluffy, with a nice, smooth feel. And you'll need a smaller angled brush for edges.

Always wash your brushes and roller covers when you're done painting, or else you won't be able to use them again . . . and **flush**—that's the sound of money going down the drain. A little soapy water is all you need. But, hey, do your family a favor and don't do this in your kitchen sink or a pretty bathroom. Go for a garage sink or a bucket outside.

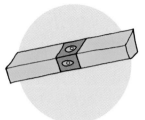

Many of the designs in this chapter involve taping, otherwise known as "masking." The tape separates the things you want to paint from the things you don't, and it provides you with a clean, straight edge. When putting the tape on the walls, you may want to use a level (a tool that tells you if you have an even line by way of a little bubble balanced in the center) or even a chalk line (a piece of string covered in chalk that you can buy at the hardware store—line it up, pull it, and **whap**, it snaps onto the wall, leaving behind a straight, faint blue line).

If you're doing any fancy masking, do not use tape from the dollar store to tape off your edges. Purchase actual painter's tape from an actual painting department of an actual hardware store or paint shop. It's designed specifically for the purpose of keeping paint out. And remember, when you're taping the walls, press firmly along the edges of the tape to get that clean line you're looking for. It will still come off when you're all done. Promise.

Yo, paint stains. So protect your clothes, carpet, shoes, and other odds and ends by investing in some cheap-o plastic drop cloths (available at paint and hardware stores) and covering everything **except** those walls. Be sure to dress in clothes and shoes you don't care about, lest they catch some paint!

A Plethora of Design Options

So once you choose your color du jour and you nab your supplies, it's time to think design. There are a myriad of ways you can paint your room. Just using one color on your walls comes to mind. Then there are painting stripes, painting each wall a different color, or painting two walls one color and a third another. Here are some methods for your madness.

Painting of any kind requires good planning and set-up. Here is an easy reference list of the things you'll need to make your paint job painless and pretty:

. . . .

What You Need

- Good painter's tape

- Assorted brushes (chosen for their paint type appropriateness)

- Roller and roller covers (chosen for the type of walls you are painting, i.e. rough, smooth, or in-between)

- A long handle for the roller (in case your ceilings are hard to reach)

- A sturdy ladder

- A paint try and plastic disposable liners

- Drop cloths galore

- Old clothes

- A pencil (for marking lines on the wall)

- A level for making level straight lines (*optional)

- A yardstick for making unlevel straight lines (*optional)

- And don't forget the paint! You'll want a latex paint. (Stay away from oils—they stink and have toxic fumes). Paint comes in various degrees of shine: High-gloss is easiest to clean but shows every wall imperfection. Semi-gloss is still easy to clean with less shine. Eggshell is next and it's perty with only a slight sheen. Flat is cool—no shine—but the hardest to keep clean.

How much paint do I need?

1 gallon covers 400 square feet

1 quart covers 100 square feet

Project #1:
The 1-2-3-4 Walls Paint Job

If your room, like most rooms, has four walls, try picking two
or three colors from the same family—colors that are just a shade
apart from one another (and usually on the same paint card at the
hardware store)—and paint each wall a slightly different color.
It lends a subtle intrigue to your room without sending you over
the deep end into clown-color mania.

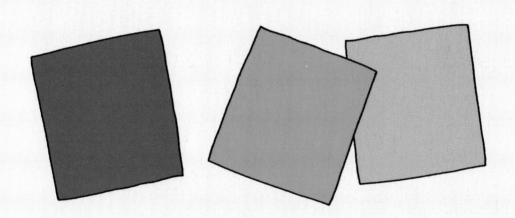

Project #2: The Single or Multiple Vertical Stripes

You've seen vertical stripes on every home improvement show on basic cable, and there's a reason. They're pretty wild, dramatic, and, though time-consuming, not too hard to create. You don't have to do a whole room; try just one wall. Also try varying the size of the stripes, so they are not uniform. You can even get the same shade of paint in two different formats—say, one glossy and one flat—and then alternate shiny stripe, flat stripe, shiny stripe, flat stripe. Or just do one wide stripe in a contrasting color. Simple and effective.

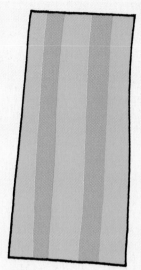

Project #3: The Zooma-Zooma Racing Stripe

More stripes. But this time think horizontal. As in racing stripes. Try painting the walls a basic color and then taping off a single fat horizontal stripe and a slimmer stripe beneath the fat one.

Sleek!

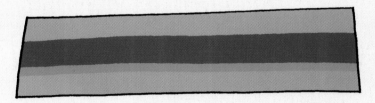

Project #4:
The Pattern Stripe, à la Gutter Art

Here we have even more stripes, but these are stripes that, when looked at closely, reveal a small pattern. How can you get this way cool effect? By using little things called "plastic gutter guards."

"What?" you say!

Plastic gutter guards, alternately known as "leaf guards," actually look a little like stencils you'd pay big money for in an art store, but they cost about a dollar. And the patterns, **oh!** On a recent trip to the hardware store I spotted a stripe made of a small diamond pattern, another made up of ovals, and yet another made up of small circles. If you taped one to the wall and painted over the cutouts, you'd end up with a 4- to 5-inch-wide stripe consisting of little paint shapes!

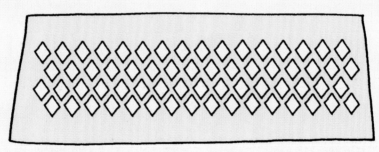

Project #5:
The Paint Card Stripe

I don't know about you, but I love, love, love the paint cards from the hardware store. If you do too, you could try painting the paint card on the wall in the form of a giant floor-to-ceiling stripe. Decide what you want the stripe to look like and then measure the height of your wall. If your paint card of choice has four colors on it, divide your stripe on the wall into four parts. Measure down from the ceiling and tape across your stripe horizontally, creating four boxes. Pick up a quart of each color on your card. Paint the colors in the boxes in the order that you see on the card. It's not just wall paint—it's art!

Project #6:
The Two-Tone Room Split

Simply cut the room in half, horizontally. Paint everything below the tape a darker color and everything above the tape a lighter or brighter color. This really requires no more effort than repainting your room one solid color, and the effect will be far more dramatic.

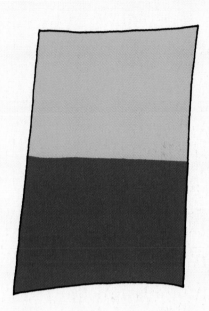

Project #7: The Imaginary Paint Frame

Paint your room one color and then tape off a large rectangular box above your bed or dresser. Paint the inside of the taped-off box with a darker or brighter color. When dry, center picture frames within the painted box or simply pin up magazine clippings or postcards with straight pins within the colorful rectangle.

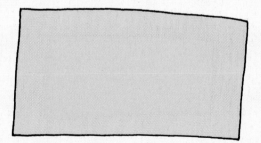

Project #8: The Imaginary Headboard

Simply paint a "mock headboard"—which is essentially just a rectangle of wood at the head of your bed, anyway—onto the wall! Tape off the same width as the head of your bed on the wall. This is the base of your headboard. Then tape a rectangle, extending as high on the wall as you want your headboard to go. Paint. Let dry. Push bed against painted wall. Voilà, new bed!

Project #9: The Cartoon Talk or Thought Bubble

Chalkboard paint now comes in both paint-on and spray paint varieties. You can obviously tape off a rectangle and paint it with the chalkboard paint, creating an oversized canvas for your chalk art. Or you could paint a cartoon bubble with your chalkboard paint, let's say over your bed or over a chair. Simply paint the bubble freehand with a brush or create a large stencil for the spray paint.

To make a stencil, pick up some contact paper at the grocery store or supermart and sketch out your design. Cut out the design with scissors and stick it to your wall. Spray paint over the cutout hole and remove the contact paper from the wall. Draw or write in the bubble a favorite saying or obsession with your chalk. Instant (and changeable) art!

Project #10:
The Contact Paper Stencil

Stenciling with contact paper in the aforementioned manner isn't limited to chalkboard paint. You can cut out all sorts of designs and stick the paper to the wall, then paint over the cutout designs with a brush, roller, or a can of sprayable stuff. Simple shapes and basic silhouettes are easiest. Think circles, bold graphic flowers, lightning bolts (for a very '80s-style effect), numbers or letters, and simple animal shapes, like a deer or a hummingbird. For the latter, print out a picture you like and blow it up on a copier to the size you want. Then cut around the edges of the picture, creating a silhouette. Use this as a guide for cutting on your contact paper. And away you go!

Project #11:
The Overhead Projector Mural

Want the Eiffel Tower on your wall? A Paul Frank monkey?
A giant palm tree? You could draw it and paint it in freehand,
but there is a little school secret that will help you pull it off
with ease: the overhead projector. Has your teacher used one of
these lately? Y'know, the lighted
box with a metal arm reaching
over the glass? Essentially,
this machine projects a
small image onto a wall,
enlarging it as it shines.
We can do the same
thing at home, with a
picture we want on our
walls, thereby giving
us a pattern to "trace."

Overhead projectors can be rented
(look up "Audiovisual Supplies" in the
Yellow Pages), and they are also
widely available in thrift stores. You
could even ask a teacher if you could
borrow one for the weekend.
(It could happen.)

There are smaller, semi-affordable overhead projectors, often called "art projectors" or "tracers," available for purchase at many art stores, too—but they'll cost you about thirty bucks. Anyhow, there are many options! You will also need a transparency of the image you want to paint. This isn't as hard as it sounds. Copy shops can photocopy an image onto a transparency for the price of a color copy. Choose an image that isn't too complex for your first go.

Make sure the projector is stable. Place the transparency on the machine and project it onto your wall. You can change the size, making the picture big or small by adjusting the projector or moving the whole machine closer or farther away. Once it's projecting the image at the size you desire, take a pencil and trace along the lines onto your wall. You may have to stand off to the side of the projector's glare and stretch your arm a bit to be able to trace some of the image. Once you have finished, turn the machine off and paint. Just try to stay within the lines!

Project #12: The Word Wall

This will take all day. Maybe several days. Ah, but the drama of the finished product!

When choosing your paint color for this project, you could go for wild and bright, or you could choose a color just two shades lighter or darker than the existing color on your walls for a serene and subtle yet wowing effect.

First, create vertical lines on the wall with a yardstick, tape measure, or chalk line. The aforementioned level would be put to good use here, but, hey, it's not a must-have. Write out the lyrics to your favorite song or poem on a piece of paper. Or better yet, write your own. Cut stencil letters into individual "tiles," then tape them together to form the first word. Continue with the second and third words, as far as you can go before you run out of the letters you need. Tape the words you've created to the wall, squared up on the line, as if the wall were a giant piece of writing paper.

Next, paint over the stencil, taking care not to paint over the edges of the stencil. After you've covered it in paint, remove the stencil from the wall. When the stencil has dried, you can take the letters apart and create the next several words in sequence. Continue this process until you've written out the entire song or poem, or until you just can't continue any longer.

Beyond Paint

Do the paint fumes make you swoon (and not in a good way?).
Do you just hate painting? Then here are a few fixes for your
bland walls.

· ·

Project #13: Giant Sticker Art

In the last year several companies have come out with supercool
oversized vinyl stickers in groovy graphic shapes, animal
silhouettes, and even scenic landscapes. They're mostly on the
costly side, but we can create our own with a little thing called
"contact paper."

I've mentioned contact paper already,
but I'll tell you more about it. Contact
paper is generally used to line kitchen
cupboard shelves. It is essentially a
roll of vinyl paper backed
with a craft paper
that you remove to
reveal a very sticky
side. It comes in
a host of colors
and patterns,
and it is available
at drugstores and
grocery stores.

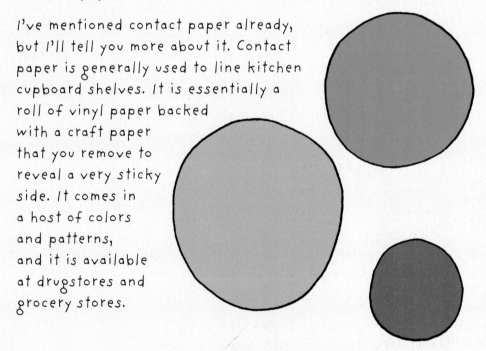

best selection is to be had at the big superstores, like Kmart, Wal-Mart, and Target. My grandmother Ruthie was obsessed with contact paper, and once, she even covered our fridge in the stuff because she wanted to give it a "new" look.

You see where I get this obsession from, no?

Oversized circles would be the easiest to make, but depending on how much of a daredevil you are, you could get mighty intricate and cut out retro-modern asteroids or sublimely sweet flowers or even a whole beach scene.

Let the contact paper display be your inspiration. Maybe you'll see a particular shade that reminds you of a meadow and—**bam!**—that inspires you to make a pasture with horses and ducks, too. But first, for the basic how-to, let's concentrate on the plain but excessively cute polka dot.

What You Need

- Contact paper in one or more groovy colors

- Scissors

- A large dinner plate, a medium-size dinner plate (or salad plate), and a smaller bread plate

- Pencil

- Some heavy books

The HOW-TO

Roll the contact paper out flat, craft paper side up, and anchor each end with a heavy book. Place your largest plate down on the paper and trace around the edges with your pencil. Remove this plate to reveal a perfect circle. Repeat this with the same plate a couple of times, then repeat it with the smaller plates as well.

Slowly and carefully cut out each circle. When you have finished cutting them all out, imagine how you want them arranged on the wall. Start with a large circle and slowly peel back just the top of the dot; affix that to the wall, smoothing it out to the edges. Then pull the rest of the paper off in a downward motion, again smoothing out the vinyl sticky part until the whole dot is on the wall and free of any bubbles or wrinkles. Repeat this all over the wall, creating a free-form pattern of polka dots.

Contact paper is very forgiving. If you don't like the placement of your circles, or if they wrinkle, just pull the sheets off and start again! That's why this is the perfect craft for you gals who have parents who aren't too into you painting your room.

Project #14: Wacky Wallpaper

Wallpaper is boring. Or rather, **most** wallpaper is boring. You know whose wallpaper isn't boring?

The fishes'.

The hamsters'.

The snakes'.

That's right. Pet store wallpaper rocks.

The photographic scenes that make up pet store wallpaper are intensely beautiful ocean and desert scenes. It's sold by the foot and has no glue because it's two-sided, since it's intended to go on glass. Most pet stores, big and small, carry this stuff. Check the fish or reptile departments.

You can tack it up "temporarily" with removable gum glue, the kind that's sold in sticks—you simply pull off a chunk and stick it to the wall. For a more permanent solution, you will need to glue the paper to your wall with a basic wallpaper glue, found at most hardware stores. You could do a whole wall, or simply stick on a stripe along one wall. You could cover your door in the paper, or you could create a faux window by cutting out just a square and placing it at eye level.

You could go one step further: Pick up an old window frame at an architectural salvage yard and cut and paste the pet store wallpaper into the glass panes. Hang the whole thing up on your wall (get some help, those windows can be heavy), and you've created a window to a whole new world, right in your own bedroom.

CHAPTER TWO

make art, not war

There's nothing worse than plain ol' white walls. **BOOORING**. Art those walls up, I say!

Wall art doesn't have to be limited to posters. Trash anything that features a member of a boy band. Discard the cartoon posters. It's high time you (effortlessly) crafted your very own, one-of-a-kind art that reflects you and your new room! Throw away any and all preconceived notions that art is all about framed paintings à la a museum (although that **can** be cool). The following projects require *less* time than it takes to drive to the mall and purchase another cheesy poster.

Project #1:
Black-and-White Gallery

Do you have a particularly large and empty wall just aching for art? This project can be as small or large as need be. Fill your entire wall, or simply make a statement with a single row of giant "framed" pictures.

But frames are expensive, right?

Wrong! We're not framing with traditional frames. We're framing with colored tape.

Where do you get colored tape? Most large-scale art stores carry the stuff in terrific shades, like orange, hot pink, and sky blue. And then there is a wondrous thing called "electrical tape." It comes in a host of different colors so that an electrician or a do-it-yourselfer can color code and differentiate various wires. The color palette includes a lovely burgundy, a subtle lilac, and a vibrant teal blue! Then, if you head from the electrical aisle over to the insulation aisle of your friendly hardware store, you are likely to find a way cool metallic silver tape, otherwise known as "aluminum" or "foil tape." Any of these tapes would work— you could even double up and use two shades or two types!

What You Need

- A handful of favorite photos

- A ride to the copy shop

- Colored tape

The How-To

Go to the copy shop, look for the color copier (they are nearly all color these days), and place your photo on the glass. You want to blow it up—most machines will let you go as large as 400 percent, and I've found that works great for standard 3 x 5 pix. Choose the black-and-white setting on the machine. (Yes, I know I told you to find a color machine, they print better; but you still want that dramatic black-and-white look.) Press the COPY button, then watch as your friends, family, and dog come out larger than life. You can mess around with the positioning, but unusual cropping is part of the art of it. Don't be afraid to take off an ear or the top of a head. While at the copy shop, take advantage of free supplies—trim your photo to a neat 10½ x 14 inches for a standard large print, or go your own way with a quirky new size. Either way, trim your print with the shop's paper cutters.

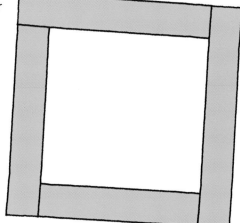

Once home, frame your photo while simultaneously affixing it to the wall with your colored tape. You can be precise and trim the tape to frame the photo perfectly with sharp corners and clean lines, or you can let caution go by the wayside and simply rip the tape ends for an edgier look. Either way, the pictures are "framed" and look far fancier than your average poster.

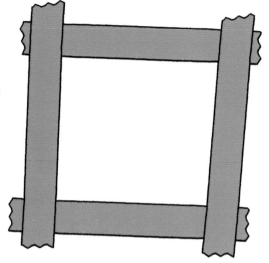

Alternate Idea #1: If familial photos are simply just too sappy for your taste, you could copy any number of things instead. Weird celebrities from the 1980s, cropped Picasso-style. Odd modern art from books you own. Newspaper articles. The pattern on the cool scarf you recently picked up from your neighborhood thrift shop. Whatever.

Alternate Idea #2: You can also have a single photo blown up really, really big at your neighborhood copy shop. It's not particularly cheap, but if you pick the right photo, it could become your most prized possession. To keep it looking more like a fantastical painting and less like a poster, try folding it round a large canvas from the art store, wrapping the edges around the back side, and stapling the poster on. Fold the corners like you would a present, and the poster will be smooth and pretty.

• • • •

Project #2:
Abstract Modern Masterpieces

Do not be scared by the following: This project involves crayons. But unlike the cute drawings you made when you were five that your mom attached to the fridge with magnets, this end result is chic.

What You Need

- A cookie sheet

- Tinfoil

- A box of crayons

- A couple sheets of watercolor paper or some textured art paper

The HOW-To

Cover one side of the cookie sheet in tinfoil. Place the cookie sheet in the oven and heat at 400 degrees for ten minutes. Pull the cookie sheet out of the oven carefully with pot holders and set it on a surface that will not burn, like the top of your stove or a trivet.* Quickly make a design on the tinfoil utilizing the crayons. Draw a simple shape or just doodle. Do not be alarmed—the crayon will melt. Use colors that are in your room or that accent things in your room. When you have finished your "drawing," place the piece of art paper on the tinfoil and press. Lift off and voilà—a beautiful abstract "painting" made unassumingly from crayons! It will dry in a matter of minutes and look like a fancy and terribly expensive oil.

To create another, just cover the cookie sheet with a new piece of tinfoil and place it back in the oven for a couple of minutes. Then repeat. You can use another piece of paper, or you can use the "print" you already made, creating a layered affect. Trim and then frame your pieces in simple black frames, purchased inexpensively from a discount store. This is also a good use for those glassless frames you may have picked up secondhand at a thrift store, because—like real oil paintings—these don't need glass. Your paintings have texture.

Don't forget to sign them!

❊ what's a trivet?

They're those weird metal things grandmas seem to have around that appear to have no utilitarian purpose whatsoever. But they are in fact used to set a hot dish on so that it doesn't ruin a table or tablecloth.

Project #3:
canvas collages

You can purchase stretched canvas at most art stores. What that means is that the material (the canvas) has been pulled tight over a wooden frame and secured, usually with staples. This provides a smooth surface to paint upon. Stretched canvases come in a wide variety of sizes, from teeny-tiny (like 3 inches by 4 inches) to very large (5 feet by 6 feet).

You don't have to limit yourself to using just paint on canvases. By combining paint with other printed materials, you can create one-of-a-kind "art" without much painting talent.

What You Need

- A canvas, any size (or two, or three, or four—but wait, let's start with one for now)

- Acrylic paints

- Paintbrush

- A cup of water

- Color photocopies of images you like (you can get these out of a book at the library, a book in your parents' own stash, a textbook, or an old magazine lying around)

The How-To

With your brush, cover the whole canvas with paint. You could paint one solid color, or you could paint a pale pattern.

Cut out the images you want to include and then place them down on the canvas. You won't need glue if the paint is still a little wet and sticky. Try positioning the image to one side or to a corner, rather than in the middle.

Now take your paint and brush and make an abstract design around your image. You could make concentric circles that get bigger or smaller as you encircle your image. Or you could paint well-defined or loose stripes. You could paint a graphic symbol, layering over it with the same symbol in a different color. You could paint a background color and then paint words or the lyrics to your favorite song. You could go for the Jackson Pollock look and splatter the paint across the canvas. But if you try this tactic, be careful to cover your surroundings with an old sheet so you don't splash paint everywhere.

Feel free to layer various colors, textures, and patterns on your canvas. Or keep the picture simple and monochromatic. Let it dry thoroughly before attempting to hang it on your wall.

Variation: I picked up a handful of really cool old sewing patterns at the thrift shop. But I didn't know what to do with them. Voilà, I made them into art, substituting the photocopy with my sewing patterns.

You could also add glitter or sequins to your painting when it's wet to create some dimension and sparkle.

Alternate Idea: This is simpler, involves even less work, and looks equally good. Simply paint your canvas a solid color. Perhaps you have three canvases—paint each a different color. Or add just a little white to your original paint color and paint the second canvas just one shade lighter than the first, and then add more white paint and paint the third canvas a shade lighter than the second. Hang on the wall. Watch as people admire your very modern art!

•   •   •   •

Project #4: Fabric as Art

Found a fantastic piece of vintage fabric at the local thrift?
Or perhaps you have an old pillowcase you love and want
to showcase, front and center. Stick it on the wall, nice
and perty!

What You Need

- A scrap of fabric—any size—that you adore

- A canvas from an art store (pick a canvas that not only can
  be completely covered by your fabric scrap, but that also is an
  appropriate size for your room)

- Stapler

The HOW-TO

Iron the fabric flat. Lay the fabric out on the floor, right side facing down. Center the canvas, front facing down, over the fabric. Pull the fabric over one edge and staple once along the wood frame on the back side. Pull the opposite side taut, but not so tight that you cause the fabric to stretch out of shape. Staple that side once to the wood edge.

Now the fabric is stapled in two places exactly opposite from each other. Two edges have no staples in them yet. Do those next.

Once you have four staples in, one on each side of the frame, it's time to start pulling and stapling all the way around. Keep checking the front, making sure the fabric is still smooth and unwrinkled. When you've stapled around the whole thing, trim the excess fabric, add a picture hanger hook or sawtooth hanger (from the hardware store, costs pennies) to the back, and hang the picture up proudly.

Ten-minute art!

• • • •

Project #5: Hockney-esque Photo Collage

David Hockney is a British artist who became quite well known in the 1960s for his "pop art"—paintings and collages that were often inspired from the imagery of television, movies, comics, and other modern art forms. Whoa! Why the art history lesson? Because Hockney did these things called "joiners," which are basically photo collages. But one of the biggest reasons they are considered "art"—while your junior high school end-of-year dance collages really aren't—is because in the case of a joiner, dozens of photos combine to create one large image. See, the final effect is more like a painting than just a bunch of photos.

Hockney often worked with Polaroid pictures to create his joiners, and you can too. Or you could go the old-school 35 mm way or the new-school digital camera way—it doesn't really matter. But think big.

As an example, let's say you were going to do a joiner of the front of your house. You would start by taking a picture of, say, just the left bottom corner of the house. Then you'd move the camera slightly to the right and take the next "section" of your house, moving across the house's lower half and taking several pictures. Then you'd start again at the left of the house, but you'd move the camera up slightly so that you're shooting just above the first group of pictures. And you'd once again move to the right, shooting as you go. Keep shooting in these small "quadrants"; include your lawn and the sky, the driveway and the car.

Then, once you've printed your shots, assemble them together, like a puzzle, to create one very large "portrait" of your house.

I bet a lot of the component pictures that you take will be intriguing and something you never would have caught on film had you not embarked on this kooky art project. That's the beauty of such an effort. You have lots and lots of unique snapshots of ordinary beauty making up one large and dramatic image.

To display your joiner, you could simply tape it to the wall, finishing the puzzle right there on your wall with just a little double-sided tape. Or you could arrange it on a large piece of paper or wood, making it easier to move around and take with you.

Of course, if your house isn't a subject you want to memorialize in photos, just apply the same principles to any landscape, scene, or group. Enlist a friend or three to help, and you can create wildly innovative art together!

Project #6:
3-D Postcards

You're wandering around the local swap meet, and you see a stack of old postcards. **Whoa, they're cool,** you think. But someone's already written on them—sent distant hellos from Greece to Aunt Martha or sweet love notes to Arthur from Rome. So you pass them up, even though they're just a couple of dollars and—did I mention?—so crazy cool.

Next time buy them. With just a few (four, to be exact) items from the hardware store, you can make them into gallery-ready art for your new room!

What You Need

- A two-by-four (it's a standard size piece of wood) cut into 2-inch cubes (do not panic, the hardware store WILL do this for you, usually for free—just ask sweetly; you need as many cubes as you have postcards)

- 4-inch-long nails to hang said cubes into wall (you'll need as many as you have cubes—as many as you have postcards, natch)

- A hammer

- Velcro (which I believe is the duct tape of the new millennium)

- You may need one more thing. If your postcards are of the flimsy sort (extra thin or delicate), it would behoove you to glue them to a piece of sturdier cardboard and trim—this way, they will last longer.

The HOW-TO

If you have some of that wall paint lying around, you could paint the wood cubes to match the wall. But frankly, if this step just seems tiresome to you, skip it. Now, take nail in hand and hammer the cubes (one nail, right in the center) to the wall. Do this in an "artful" way:

You could make a straight horizontal line.

Or a vertical one.

You could make a grid, three across and three down.

Or two rows of three.

It all depends on the empty space you have and the number of pretty postcards you've collected. Take out a ruler to make sure the distance between cubes is even, with enough room to accommodate the postcards. If you have a level, you could even get all technical and make sure they're all superstraight. Or you can wing it, using that keen eye of yours! Leave about 1½ inches between postcards (not the cubes, the postcards, so measure accordingly).

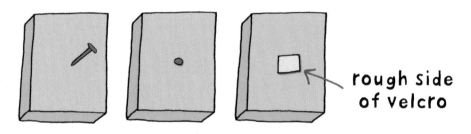

rough side of velcro

Lay each postcard facedown and apply the fuzzy side of the Velcro to the back center. Stick the rough strip of Velcro on the cube of wood. Attach card to cube.

fuzzy side of velcro

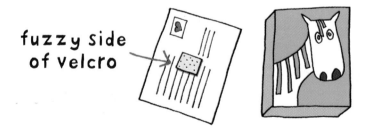

If you haven't figured this out yet, I've gone the Velcro route so that the next time you come across another beautiful set of postcards, you can—presto change-o—swap out the Rome cards for the heirloom flower cards or whatever new cards have taken your fancy!

Project #7: Thrift Art

Ever looked in the art section of a thrift store? A lot of it looks like it belongs on motel walls, but a lot of it is truly unique and lovely. Unknown artists who toil away in their garage can and do often create works of real substance. The key to buying your art at thrift shops is to come up with a theme and then purchase accordingly.

For instance, there are an awful lot of clown paintings in the world. What if you went on a mission to purchase all the cheap clown paintings you could find? Once home and in your room, you could group them together to create an "installation" of sorts, a genuinely impactful statement! Perhaps one of the solo paintings would have looked pitiful, but when paired with other kindred spirits, it shines.

other possible themes for you to "collect":

- Old Western paintings, cowboys and ranches

- Paintings of women

- Portraits

- Paint-by-number pieces

- Ballet paintings

- Seaside landscapes

- "Big-Eye" paintings (images of little kids with oversized eyes, often referred to as "Keanes" or "Keane-like" after the famous 1960s painter Walter Keane, who in fact didn't even paint the pictures that feature his name—his wife did!)

- Paintings of horses

- Paintings of dogs

To make your collection even more "of a piece," you could paint all the frames the same color. You could even add beads or ribbon to the frames with a little basic glue.

You can group them together in a very mathematically perfect grid. Or you can put them on your wall in a straight line, all the tops of the frames or all the bottoms of the frames lined up evenly. Or you can just group them tightly and randomly in a bunch on your wall.

And if the paintings are on canvas (as opposed to a print), whenever you get bored with them, you can buy this stuff called "gesso" at the art store and paint right over the old paintings, giving you blank canvases to create something wholly new.

• • • •

Project #8:
Display the Ordinary

When you group ordinary, everyday items
together, they take on a whole new meaning—
they're art! A single purse hung on the wall is
fine, if it's a truly beautiful purse. But imagine
if you hung all your so-so **and** your coolest
purses on the wall together. The grouping is
striking, visual, and graphic. Simply pick up a
box of nails at the local hardware store and
nail them into the wall, arranging the purse
straps on them as you go.

You can display your hats and necklaces in
the same manner with a similar effect. You
can also do this with any "collection" you may
have amassed. Old board games make terrific
art, especially when you have a wall of them.
You can nail them directly to the wall, or you
can purchase picture-hanging kits at the
hardware store. Follow the directions, affixing
two hooks and wire to the back of the game
boards and then hanging them up as you would
fancy framed paintings. Cool old record jackets,
pulp fiction paperback covers, old comic books—
they can all be hung in groups on your wall for
maximum effect.

Photo Finish

Photos of your friends are dear to you, right? But how to display them? Sure, there is the requisite corkboard, but you're crafty, you can go a step beyond that. Here are two ways to frame and display the best sides of your friends and family.

• •

Project #9: Mismatched to Matched in a Flash

Frames are one of those things that are plentiful at every thrift store across America and are always way cheap. But alas, they don't exactly match the frames in your room or even the other frames in the shop. Here's a quick fix.

What You Need

- A bunch of frames—they need not have anything in common except that they are all in decent shape

- A can of spray paint (should match the décor in your room: if you're going for a modern look, choose black; if you're style is pretty-pretty, maybe choose white; and if your room is just wild, perhaps you should choose a hot pink shade—but the deal is, you should pick only one shade and stick with it)

- A cool roll of wrapping paper or a large sheet of supercool paper from an art store (should also match the theme or décor of your room, and it should match the shade of paint you chose above)

- Double-sided tape

The HOW-To

Take the glass panels out of all the picture frames and put them somewhere safe. Take all the cardboard backing pieces out and set them aside; you'll need them in a moment. Take the frames outside and spread them out on some newspaper. Spray paint them lightly and wait for them to dry, then spray on another second, light coat.

Meanwhile, take your cardboard pieces and lay them out on your wrapping paper. Trace around each piece of cardboard and cut out the paper.

When the frames are dry, bring them inside. Tack down the piece of wrapping paper to the corresponding cardboard with double-sided tape. Then center your photo (or photos—you can easily put two or more small pictures in a large frame) on the wrapping paper and affix them where you want with a little double-sided tape. The paper looks like a "mat," but you didn't have to cut out anything fancy.

Put the glass back in the frame, then add the wrapping paper/cardboard/photo concoction and secure. Repeat with the other frames. Now you have a "matching set," thanks to the paint and paper!

Doodad It:

You can frame the photos on the wrapping paper with a little bit of ribbon or rickrack (that squiggly ribbon trim). Cut the ribbon into four pieces per photo, each the length of a side of the photo. Next, take the double-sided tape and affix it to all four edges of the photo, on the back side, with just a fraction of an inch peeking out on the front. Place the photo where you want it on the wrapping paper and press. Take your ribbon pieces and press them down along the edges of the tape. Put the frames back together, and voilà, you have extra-fancy matching frames.

● ● ● ●

Project #10:
Record Jacket Frames

When I was really broke but wanted to display my photos of friends and family on my walls, I turned to the filthy record store aisle in my neighborhood thrift (why are old records always so dirty?). I perused the shelves for the silliest covers I could find: Hawaiian luau music, all-boy choirs, a grandma-and-grandpa-like couple sidled up to a grand piano—you name it. If it was wacky (and cheap, fifty cents or less!), I bought it.

What You Need

- Wacky cheap record covers, all the better if the vinyl record itself is thrashed

- Scissors

- Tape

- Hole punch and some ribbon (optional)

The HOW-TO

Remove the back of the record jacket by simply cutting along the seams. Trim the front of the album cover to a size and shape that is manageable and works with the picture on it. You can cut the name of the band off or leave it on.

If the record album has faces on it, I would cut out one of the faces with my scissors (making it like a frame) and then place a photo of my friend behind the cover. Or you can put your friends "next" to the people on the cover by cutting out a hole (smaller than the actual photo, so they can "peek" through) near the people on the cover.

Of course, if your cover is just a scenic shot, then cut your rectangle or square hole accordingly, allowing your friends to "hang out" in the Hawaiian tropics or wherever (there were a lot of Hawaiian records put out in the '50s and '60s, so it doesn't take much effort to turn up a few old luau LPs).

Here's what you do. Tape the photo facedown to the back side of the record jacket so it's peeking out of the hole, then admire your work. That's it.

You can simply tape the "frame" to the wall. You can create a "stand" for the frame by cutting a triangle from the scrap cardboard of the cover, folding the edge of one side, and taping it to the back of the picture like a traditional desk frame. Or you can punch holes in each top corner of the frame and string it up from the ceiling with a piece of ribbon.

Alternate Idea: The very same process can be applied to cool old book covers, which you can find at the secondhand bookstore, or even—and this is the cheapest method of all—to cereal boxes!

• • • •

CHAPTER THREE

look, out the window!

- -

As those of us without a window in our room know, windows are wonderful things. But there is that pesky morning light to contend with. Leaving them bare just isn't an option. Introducing...

- -

Project #1: The Instant No-Sew Curtain

Curtains can be costly, but you don't have a sewing machine. So how can you make them? Hey, no problem.

What You Need

- A piece of lightweight fabric 4 inches wider and 2 inches longer than your window, cut in half to create two equal-size panels

- Fusible web tape (see page 67)

- An iron

- Two to three pieces of felt in a color that coordinates with the fabric

- Four to eight pairs of costume post earrings, like faux pearls (check the dollar stores in your area)

- A hanging curtain rod

The HOW-TO

With the fusible web tape and your iron, make a 1-inch hem on all four sides of each panel.

Cut felt pieces into strips anywhere from 8 to 16 inches long, each with one pointed end and one squared-off end. The number of strips depends on how wide your window is, but the number should be even. Gather half the felt strips, your first panel, and a handful of post earrings. Fold a felt strip in half and put it on the top of the curtain panel (an inch from one end), with the pointed end on the front and the squared-off end lined up with the point, but in the back, essentially creating a loop. Secure it by poking the post earring through the first layer of felt, then the curtain panel, and then finally through the last layer of felt. Attach the back of the earring.

You are creating the loops that will allow you to hang your curtains from the rod. You want them spaced out rather evenly along the top edge of the curtain. To do this, make your next loop on the other top end of the curtain, then space the remaining loops out between the two ends. Repeat the whole process on the other curtain panel.

Take the curtain rod off of its brackets and push the rod through the felt loops of both of your curtain panels. Hang the rod back up, and there you have it: new curtains in about an hour!

Doodad It

Felt is great because it doesn't fray and it's easy to cut. You could make the curtain loops fancier by cutting out small flower shapes in additional contrasting colored felt and poking your earring posts through these first, before you stick them through the loops and curtain panel. If flowers aren't your thing, how about geometric shapes? Banner flags? Stars? Shells?

Doodad It Deux

For a little more style and a lot more coverage, use two layers of complementary fabric, but hem the top layer slightly shorter than the back layer so the back layer peeks out.

Alternate Idea: If your quest for cool (and cheap) post earrings leaves you heartbroken, you could hand sew an X stitch (officially called a "cross-stitch") where the earring would have gone with a large needle and embroidery floss. But wear a thimble to save your thumb the pain of pushing through three layers of fabric! Not quite "no-sew," but "sew" close, no?

• • • •

Project #2: Shower curtain curtains

C'mon, they're a natural. Shower curtains already have holes in the top for rings, so they effortlessly slide onto a shower bar or—you got it!—a curtain rod. And most of the plastic jobs are pretty darn cheap.

Plastic, since it's not technically a fabric, isn't going to fray, so you can cut it to the size you need. You can also paint on it pretty easily with acrylic paint, decorating your "curtain" in the colors of your room. And even though it isn't a fabric, you can still sew things to it: plastic or silk flowers, sequins, plastic bubble gum charms, ball fringe—you name it.

My favorite shower curtain curtain is cheap and simple, but it's a little time-consuming to make. Turn the stereo on and hunker down in your room for a while, and in no time you'll have a cool curtain like no other.

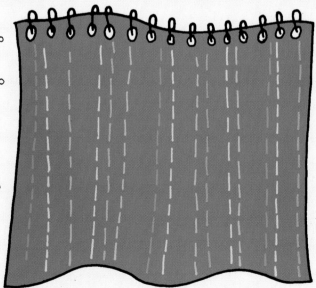

What You Need

- A very cheap plastic shower curtain in any color, cut to the size of your window and complete with shower rings

- Very thin, dense yarn in colors that will match your room (keep your eye out at thrift stores, where you can pick up whole skeins for a quarter)

- One needle large enough to thread yarn through

- Washable marker

The How-To

Spread the curtain out flat on the floor. Sketch out a design on the shower curtain with your marker. Starbursts are fun and easy. Straight, unevenly placed vertical lines are modern and will provide a lot of coverage. You can even write out something in cursive script, like **j'taime** or **Sunlight, Sunbright** or something that is so very you.

a mini tip:

Spray your curtains with a touch of body spray or your favorite perfume, open up those windows, and let the scent waft into your room oh-so-delicately. Heaven!

Thread your needle with a long piece of yarn, knot the end, and "embroider" your shower curtain, starting from the back side. It's best to tie off your yarn after you finish each design element rather than just making long stitches on the back of the curtain, because they will show through when the light comes through your window. Use different colors of yarn or keep it monochromatic. Either way, the end result will be a curtain unlike anyone else's, and what did it cost? A couple bucks, tops.

Alternate Idea: If your curtain is lacking a rod altogether but your window is recessed, you can pick up an adjustable-width shower rod for just a few dollars and wedge it into the top of the recessed window for an instant curtain rod.

• • • •

Project #3: The card curtain

Who says curtains have to be made of fabric? Not me. This project incorporates cards into a curtain. Cards? Yes, as in playing cards or flash cards or even your stash of favorite greeting cards (as long as you trim them all to the same size). This is a great project for vintage or vintage-looking gin rummy cards. And although it is time-consuming, it's worth every minute.

What You Need

- A whole lot of cards (how many depends on the size of the cards and the size of your window—but don't try this with a large, massive window!)

- A ¼-inch hole punch (pick one up at the craft store, natch)

- Yarn or embroidery floss

- Tape

- Scissors

- A piece of paper (or pieces of paper taped together) the size of your window

The How-To

Start by punching a hole in all four of corners of each card, **except** the cards that will be on the bottom edge of your curtain—they need holes punched only in the top left and right corners. Keep close to the edges, but make sure you get clean and complete holes.

Lay the window-size piece of paper out on your floor. Arrange the cards on the paper, making sure you have enough to cover the width and length of the window. You can leave an eighth of an inch to an inch between the cards, but make sure to leave an even amount on all sides of the cards. And keep in mind that the more space you leave between the cards, the more light you'll let in.

Cut your yarn or embroidery floss into a bunch of 3- to 4-inch pieces. Take a small piece of tape and wrap it around the ends of each piece of yarn or embroidery floss, kind of like the hard plastic bits on the ends of shoelaces. These are makeshift "needles." They make threading through the little holes you punched on the cards much easier.

Start tying the cards together, using a single piece of string for each connection. Secure each connection with a knot. You can go back and trim the knots when you are all done. Some holes will be used for two connections, but two bits of yarn will fit through even an eighth-inch hole. Take your time and work your way across and then down until you have secured all the connections.

You can attach this to your window using simple tacks. Just tack through your cards directly into the wall above your window.

Or you can use clip-on curtain rings. You can find these at most discount stores, like Target or Kmart. They have a curtain ring and a spring-loaded clip. You simply clip a ring to every other card along the top row of your curtain and hang it from a basic rod.

Or, if you have a curtain rod you'd like to attach this to but no clip-on rings, you can create yarn loops by feeding pieces of yarn through the holes at the top edge of the card curtain and knotting them off. Slide the rod through your yarn loops, and you've got a new curtain!

CHAPTER FOUR

sleep easy

• •

The bed and its accoutrements, like blankets and pillows, are the central part of your space. Without them, you'd be sleeping on the floor in a sleeping bag or perhaps in a tent (hey, now there's an idea...). So how and where you place your bed and how you adorn it are key to expressing your personality in the bedroom.

First, ask yourself if you would like your bed to function primarily as it was intended—as a bed? All fluffy and covered in pillows? Or would you rather have a mini studio apartment, with your bed doubling as a hangout zone—a couch of sorts? Perhaps you want the Zen look, with the bed as low to the ground as possible. Oh, the possibilities! Now let's make that dream bed happen....

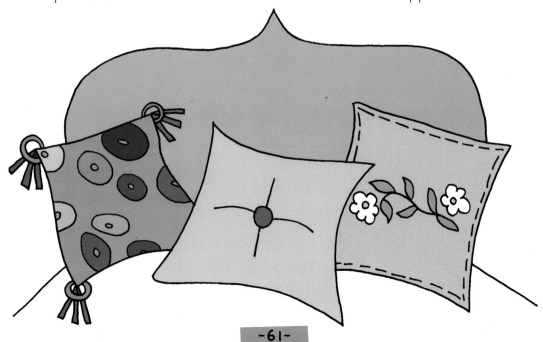

Project #1: The Girly Bed

If you have a bed frame, great. Make sure that the headboard of the bed is against a *wall* with open space on either side of the frame. If you don't have much in the way of a frame (either one of those stark metal jobs or, worse, no frame at all), don't fret. You can *still* have a girly bed a-go-go. Start with the head of the bed against a wall, as with the headboarded bed. We're gonna make it feel like a rich and elegant bed no matter what. How? With the canopy of your dreams!

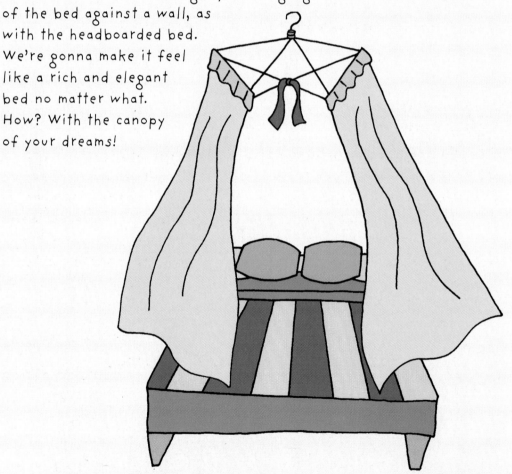

What You Need

- A screw hook

- Two wire hangers

- Six yards of inexpensive, lightweight fabric that looks good on either side; some great choices are poly chiffon, organza or mesh, and other light-as-air weaves

- A foot or more of ribbon

- Rubber band (it can be one of your hair bands)

- Needle and thread

The HOW-TO

Take one of the wire hangers and unbend the hook part till it's straight. Place this hanger through the other hanger, forming a crisscross hanger apparatus. Wrap the straight piece of hanger wire (the one that was once a hook) around the other curved top. Wrap the rubber band around the top of both hangers where they meet, binding them together. Wrap and tie the ribbon around the bottom of the hangers where they cross, further securing them in their butterfly crisscross shape.

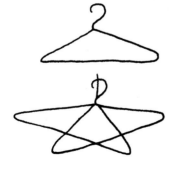

Cut your fabric into two 3-yard lengths. Take the first piece in hand with needle and thread. Use a running stitch* to create gathers along one short end. Before knotting, hold the gathered end up to your hanger contraption. You want this length of fabric to fit comfortably from one end of one hanger to the other. Fidget with the gathers till they are the right length, then knot the thread to secure them. Repeat this with the other piece of fabric.

You can sew these pieces to the hangers with a sturdy backstitch, or you can go the easier route by pinning the pieces to the hangers with a handful of safety pins. You can even weave a little ribbon around the pins to incorporate them into your "design." Pins are quite simply very secure devices and fairly effortless to use.

You may need a little help from a friend, big brother, or parent for this next part. You want to screw the rounded hook into your ceiling above the head of your bed. You don't need any tools, just a little might. Make sure you get it screwed in all the way so it doesn't come tumbling down on your head in the middle of the night.

Hang the canopy on the eye hook, positioning it so that a piece of fabric falls to each side of your bed. Leave it loose and flowy, a halo over your bed. Or you could tie back each side like a fancy window curtain with a short length of ribbon.

Doodad It

Grab a roll of fusible web tape,* an iron, and some fringe. Stick the fusible web to the bottom hem of the fabric, on the back side. Add the fringe on top of that so it hangs down beyond the hem; iron in place. Presto, instant chic glamour!

• • • •

What's a running stitch? And what is this stuff you call "fusible web tape"? The answers to these and other important questions are all in the first book in this series, the ever-magical tome, **I Wanna Make My Own Clothes**. Hey, if you don't have that book (yet!), no sweat! Here's a recap of stitching and not stitching.

There are four basic stitches that the hand seamstress must know. And one cheater method at the end.

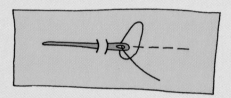

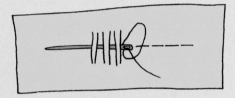

The Straight Stitch

This is the stitch that's used most often. Start by poking the threaded needle through the fabric from the underside till the knot stops you dead in its tracks. Bring the needle down into the fabric just a quarter of an inch (or even less) away from where you first poked through. Pull firmly but not tightly—you know the diff, right? Keep doing this in even increments along your seam line. Try to keep it very straight.

The Running Stitch

We use this for making gathers and lovely little, tiny pleats. It also goes by the name "basting."

You start by poking the threaded needle through the fabric from the underside, but you do not—I repeat **do not**—pull the needle all the way through. Instead, you make several little stitches right there on the needle. The point of the needle will go in the fabric and then come up the other side, keeping the stitches actually on the needle. When the needle is full (which will take anywhere from three to five full stitches), pull your needle out till the knot stops you quick. Pull your thread with a firm but gentle hand. Instant gathers!

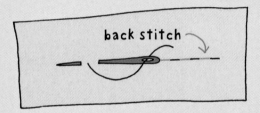

The Backstitch

This stitch is perfect when you need a supersturdy seam.

Make a single, classic straight stitch. Let's say, for example, it's a quarter inch long. Poke the needle back up through the fabric—in this case, a quarter inch past where your straight stitch ended. Now bring the needle down where your first stitch ended, essentially moving backward and closing the gap between the stitches. Repeat. It's a

forward, backward, forward, backward motion, and it makes for a nice, tight bond.

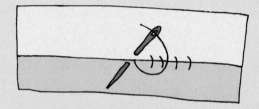

The Hemstitch

Surprise: This stitch is for hemming! As in the bottom of your curtains or the edge of a pillow.

Start by making a small fold in the fabric, hiding the raggedy raw edge. Press it with an iron. Then make another fold, once again ironing it down. Stick the point of the needle actually inside the hem and pull it through. We do this to hide the knot. Imagine the edge of the hem as a line. You want to make teeny-tiny diagonal stitches along that line. But you don't want to go through the fabric carelessly. Rather, you poke the needle through the fabric gingerly.

The goal, really, is to get only a couple of threads of the fabric with each stitch.

Push the needle back down into the hem fold, but not all the way. Pull it out from under the fold. Keep going, repeating these steps. If you keep the stitches small, you'll end up with a nearly invisible stitch on the front side. Pretty nifty, huh?

attached on both sides. Peel one side off and stick the fusible web tape along the edge of your fabric. Peel off the top layer of paper and then place the fabric or trim you want to attach to the first piece of fabric on top of the fusible web tape. Iron down on a medium setting, and it "fuses" together in seconds. How's that for a secret no-sew tip?

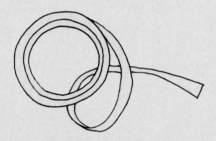

Fusible Web Tape

This magical sticky stuff is used to avoid sewing altogether. It fuses two seams together (or trim to fabric) with just the heat of a regular ol' iron. Sold at craft and fabric stores, it comes in big sheets, for attaching appliqué work, and tapelike rolls, for fusing hems. Since it is way sticky, it comes with paper

Project #2:
The Studio Apartment with Daybed

This isn't so much a "project" as it is an arrangement. Start by pushing one long side of the bed against a wall. Now you'll need pillows. Lots of pillows. (For ideas on how to make pillows, read ahead!) Classic flat sleeping pillows can line the side of the bed that is against the wall. Smaller square pillows can lean against those in "throw pillow" manner. And, if you can pull it off, bolster pillows—those long cylindrical pillows—should be at each short end, but this is not necessary.

The next step is to add a coffee table in front of the "bed/couch." You can check trash heaps, thrift stores, or your very own garage for one of these. Something smallish and low to the ground is best—unless you live in a cavernous bedroom, you probably don't have a ton of space.

It doesn't matter if the table is unattractive. You can paint it. You can decoupage it (see pages 101-105) with pictures from magazines. You can glue beads and beans and glitter to it. You can beautify it.

If a coffee table is too elusive for you, buy a cardboard box from your local packing place (or get it free from the back of a grocery store!). Just make sure it's clean. Then artfully toss a scarf, scrap of fabric, or other clothlike substance over the top covering its, um, "boxiness." Arrange a few books on top, and voilà, instant table.

Now, here is the something extra. You may meet with resistance from your folks or you may not. Remind them that it's strictly for style—it's not to serve a purpose other than that. Ready?

I'm talking about a mantel. Yes, a mantel! You'd be surprised how many fireplace mantels there are in the world that are just hanging around trash heaps, junk shops, and home salvage yards. You can even pick one up new at your local hardware emporium, but you may find it costs too much at such a store. If you find a new one, funk it up with some sandpaper and paint or even a little glue and random ceramic tiles. And if you are lucky enough to find a cool used one, just give it a good cleaning before bringing it in your room. You don't get the fireplace with it, just the groovy mantel—which will become the perfect perch for all your pals' pix. (Say that three times fast.) And it gives your modern studio apartment a whole 'nother dimension.

Once you are ready, position your mantel against a wall near your bed/couch, then ask your mom or dad to secure it to the wall for you (these things can be heavy; you don't need it falling on a big toe, or worse!).

Habitat for Humanity,

the nonprofit organization that builds houses for people in need, has shops around the country that sell used fixtures and other salvageable pieces of homes for dirt cheap, with all the proceeds going back into their way cool projects. Amid the old sinks and toilets (gross!) you'll find old chandeliers, medicine cabinets, tables, chairs, closet doodads, doors, windows, and, yes, mantels! There is a wealth of ideas inside the four walls of these shops. Check your Yellow Pages to see if you have such a fantastic shop in your neck of the woods.

A bit pricier but still inspiring are shops that specialize in architectural salvage. These places often charge antique store prices, but the goods that can be found include way old house letters and numbers (great wall décor), wacky doorknobs, vintage signs, beautiful stained glass, and, you know it, mantels! Just look up "Architectural Salvage" or just plain "Salvage" in your Yellow Pages.

Pillow Talk and Bountiful Blankies

With a scrap of fabric, needle, thread, and an hour, you too can make a pillow! Here are a handful of pillow projects.

. . . .

Project #3:
The Basic Pillow

. . . .

What You Need

- Two pieces of fabric cut to the same size and shape

- Needle and thread

- Stuffing (found at craft or fabric shop) or an old pillow with the outer fabric stripped off

The HOW-TO

Simple. Place the right sides of the fabric together, facing each other. Pin along the edges. With your needle and thread, sew a straight stitch along the edges of three sides, leaving the fourth side open. Remove the pins. Turn right side out. Slip in your stuffing or old pillow form, then sew your fourth side up using a small hemstitch. Done.

Branch out! After you've done a square and a rectangle, try your hand at a circular or triangular pillow. Same principle, different shape.

• • • •

The Pillow Form

When making a pillow, you've got lots of options. You could use stuffing—it comes in a bag and is available in polyester or cotton or a blend of sorts. Or you could use pillow forms. These are essentially uncovered pillows for sale. You can find them in every shape and size imaginable, and they make for a professional pillow silhouette. Mostly they come stuffed in the same poly blend stuffing you can buy in a bag, but sometimes you can even find pillow forms stuffed with down or a synthetic down, both of which make for truly soft pillows. In any event, using a pillow form doesn't change the pillow-making process too much, except that you have to leave a hole large enough to stuff a whole pillow through. But the end result is a nicely formed pillow.

Project #4:
The Basic Removable Pillow cover

Want a pillowcase you can remove later and wash? No sweat.

What You Need

- Two pieces of fabric the same size, except one has an extra 1½ inches on one end

- Needle and thread

- Stuffing or pillow form

- 6 inches of Velcro, cut into two 3-inch pieces

The HOW-TO

Place the right sides of the fabric together, facing each other (as for the previous project, the Basic Pillow), and pin. But this time one side of your pillow will have a longer end. Avoid that side till the end. Sew the other three sides together with a straight stitch. Remove the pins.

Now, without sewing the last side together, hem the edges using a hemstitch. Turn it right side out.

Next, add 3 inches of the rough part of the Velcro to the left, longer edge (on the wrong side of the fabric) and another strip of rough Velcro to the right edge. Fold the extra bit over the pillow and attach the fuzzy bits of Velcro where the rough bits will meet on the pillow.

Stuff the thing! Close with the Velcro. Now you can remove the pillow casing and wash it when it gets a little cola on it.

● ● ● ●

Project #5:
The Sweater Pillow

Who says you need to use material from a fabric store? You can cut up anything that has enough cool cloth to surround some stuffing. You can even use an old sweater.

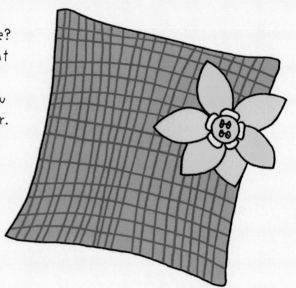

What You Need

- A cute but unwearable sweater

- Needle and thread

- Stuffing or pillow form

- A cute faux flower for decoration, with a safety-pin backing

The HOW-TO

Cut out two square or rectangular shapes from the sweater that are the same exact size. Follow the directions for the Basic Pillow. When you're finished, pin a faux flower in one corner.

Warm and fuzzy!

Project #6:
The Tee Shirt Pillow

Have a favorite tee shirt that doesn't fit anymore, but you just cannot part with it? What to do, what to do? Make a pillow out of it!

What You Need

- A great tee shirt that you don't wear

- Needle and thread

- Stuffing or pillow form

The HOW-TO

Follow the directions for the Basic Pillow, but when cutting out your shape for your pillow, try to center any cool graphic that was on the tee shirt. Supersoft and oh-so-cool, especially if said shirt was a concert tee! The possibilities are endless.

What else can you make a pillow out of? How about...

● ● ● ●

Project #7:
The Handkerchief/Scarf Pillow

Another great place to look for pillow fabric is in the scarf section of your local vintage shop. In the fifties, companies made beautiful square scarves and handkerchiefs depicting the best things about a state or country. They were usually made of silk. The colors and graphics are amazing. They would make most excellent pillows.

What You Need

- A vintage scarf
- A piece of fabric cut to the same size as the scarf**
- Pins
- Needle and thread
- Stuffing

The HOW-TO

You're going to use the same method as that for the Basic Pillow; however, you need to be extra careful with a thin, silky scarf. Keep your stitches as close as you can to the edge and take your time.

Other things to make pillows out of: jeans, cords, towels, old prom dresses, baby blankets. Even Astroturf can work. Use your imagination, and anything can become a pillow!

** Of course, you could use two scarves—one for the front and one for the back—but it's actually harder than you'd think to find two that are the same size! Try pairing your scarf with a fabric that is quite different from your scarf, like faux fur or fleece. Or stick with basic cotton, either solid or printed.

● ● ● ●

Project #8:
The No-Sew Pillow

This is the easiest route to making pillows. The catch? You really need to use fleece, or a large tee shirt would work too, but either way, you need fabric that won't unravel on the ends and that has a nice stretch. So fleece is perfect. It's way soft (perfect for pillows), and these days it comes in a variety of adorable patterns and great solids. The measurements here are for a 16-inch square pillow, but you can adapt the measurements to suit whatever size pillow you'd like.

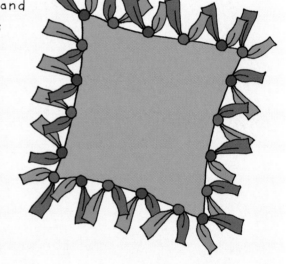

What You Need

- Two pieces of fleece (the same or different patterns or colors), each cut into a 28-inch square

- Scissors

- Stuffing or a 16-inch pillow form

The How-To

Put your squares one on top of the other. Cut a 6-inch square from one corner, cutting through both layers of fabric. Measure it out with a ruler to be reasonably precise. Then use the removed 6-inch square as your guide to cut three more 6-inch squares, one from each remaining corner.

cut a 6-inch square from each corner —→

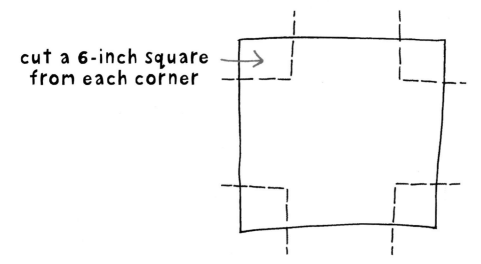

You're left with this shape:

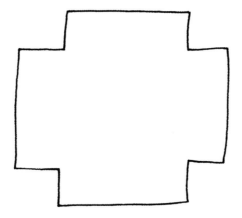

Make a cut every 1 inch for about 6 inches' worth of fabric, creating a sort of fringe. Do this along all four sides. The top and bottom sides need to have the same number of cuts. The left and right sides also need to have the same number of cuts—but don't feel obligated to make the same number of cuts as you did on the top and bottom sides. (**Whew.** Hope you got that, 'cause I am not sure I did!)

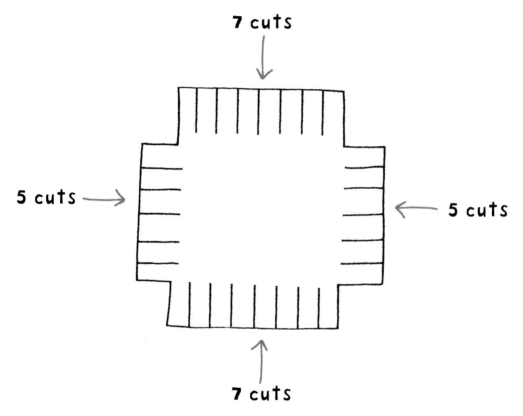

7 cuts

5 cuts →   ← **5 cuts**

7 cuts

Starting on one corner, tie the corresponding fringe from the bottom and top layers into knots all the way around the pillow, stopping when you have knotted three sides. As you tie, tug gently on opposite sides of the pillow to stretch out any bunching. Take your time; if you don't pay attention while you knot, you run the risk of knotting the wrong two pieces together!

start knotting top and bottom layers of fringe

Stuff the pillow with stuffing or the form, then knot the final side. And that's it. No needles, no thread.

I like using one patterned piece of fleece and one solid, because your fringe turns out to be a combination of both fabrics.

You can make a matching no-sew fleece blanket in the same exact way. Just cut your fabric much, much bigger. (Will it be a throw blanket? Try 1 yard of each fabric. A blanket for your bed? About 2 yards of each should be enough.) And don't worry about stuffing it! Just tie all four sides and you're done. Once you've made yourself a pillow/blanket set, make another for your best friend's birthday or for your little sister, just because.

Introduction to Felting

If you've ever had to wash your own clothes, you've probably experienced the terror of the shrinking sweater. Wool sweaters just weren't meant for the washing machine. Unless, of course, you want to do what's called "felting."

Honestly, I was scared of felting until recently. It seemed downright cruel to spend so much time creating my precious works of knitting art only to later shrink them on purpose. But then I discovered that I didn't have to do the knitting myself. I could pick up old wool sweaters at garage sales, swap meets, and thrift stores and felt **them**!

So why exactly do you wanna felt?

Once you felt a knit, you can cut it and it won't unravel. Felting meshes the knit's fibers together into something more like fabric—more like, well, what you know as felt. You can then cut it up and sew it back together into a blanket, throw, or pillow. You could even make a hat, a purse, or a cuff, but we're not concerned with those here.

Start with a sweater. (It can't be acrylic. It must be wool or mostly wool, but cashmere is in the wool family, so yes, that works, but whoa, make sure you're done with that cashmere sweater before you destroy it!) Turn the one sweater into a pillow and then, if you're happy with the results, gradually pick up more and more cheap, stretched-out, and oversized wool sweaters. Soon you'll be able to make yourself anything, even a patchwork-type blanket—warm, cozy, and stylishly chic.

* JUST ONE WARNING: Felting shrinks knits by up to 50%. The looser the knit, the more it'll shrink.

Project #9:
The Felted Pillow

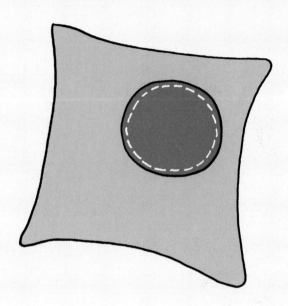

What You Need

- A wool sweater
- A washing machine
- A teeny-tiny amount of detergent
- Scissors
- Needle and thread

The How-To

Toss the sweater into the machine, add a touch of soap, and turn the washer on. A fairly long cycle with a hot wash and a cold rinse would probably be best, but you may need to do a bit of experimenting with time and temperature.

Once the cycle is **finito**, toss the shrunken sweater into the dryer for ten or twenty minutes. If you like the texture and tightness of the sweater after the first wash cycle, you can let it air dry. If you think it needs more time and more shrinkage, then wash it a second time, but for a much shorter cycle.

Once the sweater is dry, you can dismantle it with your scissors, cutting out two squares the same size for your pillow. Because the ends won't fray or unravel, you don't have to sew this type of pillow inside out. Simply stuff the pieces as if they were sewn and pin their edges all the way around. Then sew your seams ½ inch to 1 inch from the edge, all the way around. This is not only easy, it gives a nice decorative edge, too. Try cutting out the pillow shape with pinking shears (those zigzag scissors), and you'll really have a fun, flirty pillow.

Doodad It

Felt two different sweaters in contrasting colors in the manner described above. From one sweater, cut out two squares the same size, just like you did above. But on one of the squares cut out a shape from the center, like a circle or a smaller square. Take your contrasting colored felted sweater and cut a piece large enough to cover the cutout on the pillow panel.

Using embroidery floss, sew the contrasting piece to the back side of the cutout panel, following along the edges with a straight stitch. See, the color peeks through the cutout window! Stuff and sew up all four sides for a very mod pillow.

Project #10: An Easy "Quilt"

Quilting, while not exactly hard, is an art form that takes time and patience to learn. But when you don't have the time and your patience is running dry, try my fake quilting technique. It still requires some tedious sewing time, but nothing like the dozens of hours it takes to make a real quilt.

You can make this with a couple of flat bedsheets or with material you buy at the fabric store. The only thing to look out for with the latter is width—most fabric comes in 45-inch or 60-inch widths. Both sizes are fine if you have a twin bed, but anything less than 45 inches won't be wide enough for your bed, and you'll have to sew pieces of fabric together to get the appropriate width.

Oh, and batting—the stuffing stuff that's inside quilts—is sold specifically for quilts in the perfect size for your bed. Just buy it prepackaged in "twin," "full," or "queen" sizes.

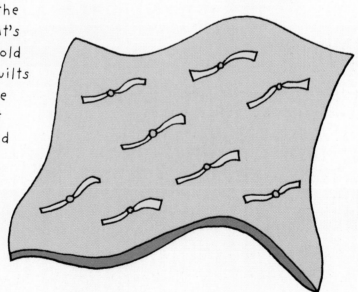

What You Need

- Two pieces of fabric (they can and should be different), large enough to cover your bed

- A roll of batting the appropriate size for your bed

- Needle and thread

- A small ball of yarn

- A second needle with an eye large enough for the yarn

The How-To

This is a lot like making a giant pillow—or a **reeeeally** big bag. Lay the two pieces of fabric out, right sides facing each other. It's going to take some time, but hand sew three sides using the basic straight stitch. Watch TV or listen to music while you sew, and the time will fly. Knot the thread and turn the cover right side out. Now that you have an enormous "pillowcase bag," unroll the batting and slip it inside. Make sure it's all nice and smooth and fits end to end. If you need to trim it to fit, just take a scissor to it.

Once it's all laid out smooth, stitch up the fourth and final side, folding the edges inward as you sew with your hemstitch. But wait, you're not done. If you were to throw this blanket on your bed in its current state, the sheet of batting would bunch up at one end. To prevent this travesty, we're going to "quick-quilt" the comforter.

One side of the comforter will show just a small tight knot; the other side will have a little bow tie. Decide which side you want to have the tie on, and for now, let's call that the top. Thread

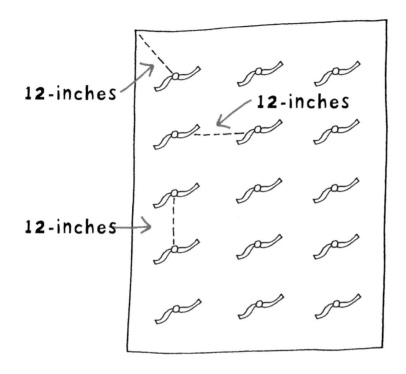

12-inches

12-inches

12-inches

the large needle with the yarn, but don't knot the end. Measure
12 inches, diagonally, from one corner of the comforter, then
poke the needle from the top, through the batting and through
the bottom layer of fabric. Come back up just a quarter inch from
where the needle poked down and pull it up through the top.
Pull the needle off the yarn, making sure not to pull the yarn out
of the comforter. Knot the two ends of yarn (or tie them into a
double knot bow) and snip the thread to the desired length (I like
about 3 inches of yarn hanging out). Repeat this process every
12 inches or so till you've secured the batting in place and made
a cute "quiltlike" pattern on your comforter.

Not only is it darling, but it's warm, too!

• • • •

CHAPTER FIVE

funkify your furniture

In this chapter you will learn a few basic tricks to make your existing furniture sing with style. And will even cover a couple of projects that allow you to "make" your own furniture, no tools required.

Nighty Nightstands

Need something new? Look to something old or something unexpected. Here are a few quick and easy "new" nightstands for you to dream by.

Project #1: The Ladder Nightstand

Two-step wood ladders are cheap and abundant. They are also the perfect height for a nightstand. Spray paint one a bright color (outside, please!) to match the décor of your room, or leave it au naturel and woodsy. Each step becomes a tabletop just perfect for holding alarm clocks, drinks, and books.

Project #2: The Sawhorse Nightstand

Wood sawhorses can be found at your local hardware store. They come in several sizes and are often used as quick makeshift tables. You take two, throw a piece of wood on them, and there you go—instant table. But that's not how we shall use them, oh, no! Pick up one—the smallest size they come in is usually 18 inches tall, and that's good for us. Set it beside your bed. It has a lovely narrow shelf top, wide enough for a clock or drinking glass, plus it has a shelf underneath—just the right size for stashing a stack of fashion magazines! Paint it or leave it alone, the choice is yours. Easy, no?

Project #3: The cable Spool Nightstand

Cable spools are available at some big hardware stores and often from your local cable company. They look just as they sound—like giant thread spools. Just stand one up next to your bed, and voilà, instant table. Toss a tablecloth or fabric scrap over it, or paint it. Either way, it's a conversation piece!

Project #4: The Skateboard Deck Nightstand

Take a skateboard deck and four premade table legs, which are available at the hardware store. They come in various sizes, from 4 inches to 28 inches tall, and cost anywhere from $1.50 to $10 apiece. They already have screws inside them, peeking out an inch. The screws are slightly larger than the holes already drilled on the skate deck, but no matter; once you get each screw started in each hole, they will screw in just fine. Just twist each leg and hold the deck steady.

You can also create a skateboard table with casters, or wheels. But these wheels are different from skate wheels because they lock in place, ensuring that your table won't roll away from you. Casters start at about a dollar apiece and come in all sorts of sizes. They even come as "tri-dollies," or three wheels on one piece of hardware, which would make for a sturdy little table.

Doorstops are another "leg" option for your skateboard nightstand. They're the little metal "sticks" with a soft tip that screw into the wall to save it from door nicks. Know what I'm talking about? They're cheap—starting at just seventy-five cents each—and they, too, have little screws already built in. You can spray paint them or buy brushed metal doorstops and leave them as is. Just make sure not to choose the coil or spring-type doorstops! Those will just crumple under the weight of the deck.

There are so many things you can do to make a plain or otherwise boring dresser into something exciting and new. Some take minutes, others take hours, but none of them take more than a day. Most of them cost pocket change, and a few may cost more, but more than a whole new dresser? No way.

. . . .

Project #5: New Knobs

Find some new ones at the local hardware store. Even the smallest hardware shops have a reasonable selection of knobs, and the superstores have aisles of choices. They don't cost a ton, and they really spruce up a dresser in an instant. And don't forget to check out the lighting aisle. Next to the pull chains there are lighting knobs, originally intended to cap off lamps. But they have screws, just like regular knobs, and they are often far more ornamental and fancy than traditional knobs. On a recent hardware store run I spotted lighting knobs in the shapes of a large brass pineapple and a Chinese fan, either of which would make exceptionally cute drawer knobs!

Find some vintage knobs at the salvage shop. They don't have to match. Mix them up, and you'll have a funky retro look for a lot less money than you'd spend for a complete matching set.

Ribbon pulls, anyone? Remove your current knobs and thread one end of short ribbon through each hole left in your drawer. Tie a large knot on the inside of the drawer. Knot the other end on the outer face of the drawer. What pretty pulls!

Or, from the outside of the drawer, push both ends of ribbon through the holes till you create a loop on the front of the drawer. Knot both ends of the ribbon together on the inside. Then sew a plastic or silk flower onto the loop to serve as a "stopper"—and as an adorable accoutrement.

Glue any number of small items to the ends of your old knobs (or cheap new knobs with flat surfaces). Dice. Those plastic magnet letters that toddlers play with. Pictures of your best friend or that star you're crushing on this month. Plastic zoo animals. Gumball-machine toys. Band buttons. Anything!

Like your knobs? Keep 'em, but add something new: tassels.

I dunno what it is about tassels, but I like 'em. They could be all stiff and stuffy, dangling from monstrous mahogany furniture in grand palaces of yore. But when made from fun-colored thread and hung on ordinary ol' furniture, they're simply supercool.

These are great to hang on your dresser knobs to make them new and exciting without taking them out. You can also slide a tassel over your doorknob or closet doorknobs, or attach some to lovely gifts for Mom or your best bud.

What You Need

- Embroidery floss
- A piece of cardboard, 8 inches long for a standard-size tassel
- Scissors

The How-To

Wind the floss lengthwise around the cardboard many, many times—at least eight, maybe more. Slip a 6-inch-long piece of floss under the wrapped floss at one end and tie it into a looped knot. Slide the floss off the cardboard and tie another 6-inch piece of floss around the top of the wrapped floss, 1 inch from the top. Knot it and trim it so you can no longer see the knot. Now cut the other end of the tassel so that there are no more "loops" on that end and they are all even. Done. Easy, peasy, pie.

•   •   •   •

Project #6:
Mirror, Mirror, on the Wall

Turn any dresser (or table or nightstand) into a dressing table with an unexpected mirror: Use an old automobile side mirror! You can pick these up at the dump, used-car lots, the auto parts store, even at thrift stores from time to time. Just screw or nail them to the sides of your dresser for handy and remarkably cute mirrors!

Decoupage

Decoupage, a twelfth-century invention, kind of got a bad rap a few decades ago, thanks to the many Girl Scouts and housewives of the 1970s who decoupaged **everything**, from napkin rings to tissue-box holders. **Très** tacky!

Essentially, decoupage is the art of gluing paper to something else, then lacquering the paper with some sort of clear glue. Today decoupage is a modern art form that can transform the plain and ordinary into something personalized and wonderful.

Things You can Decoupage

- Glass plates (you can decoupage to the underside so that the images are facing up, through the glass)

- Tin cans and tin boxes

- Glass bottles

- Tea sets

- Trays

- Jewelry boxes

- Hatboxes

- Shoe boxes

- Mailboxes

- Furniture: nightstands, wood chairs and chests, dressers, headboards

- Wood screens

- Mirror edges

- Chalkboard and bulletin board frames

- Tiles

- Heels of wooden shoes

- Vases

- Frames

- Trash cans and recycling bins

- Lamp bases and lamp shades

- Canvas

- Flowerpots

- Toilet seat lids

People have decoupaged their walls and ceilings, but once it's on there, it's on for good, so I do not—I repeat, **do not**—recommend this. Oh, and I don't recommend decoupaging everything in your room. It's simply too much for one room to take. Remember, moderation is key.

Little Bits of Decoupage = Way Cool Art

Too Much Decoupage = Ticky-Tacky

The Tools of Decoupage

- ALL kinds of paper: wrapping paper, pages from old children's books, comics, newspaper, Chinese tea paper, wallpaper, paper napkins, magazine clippings, old sewing patterns, paper bags, photocopies of photos, old textbook pages, weird biology posters—literally, anything that is made of paper or can be photocopied onto paper

- Decoupage glue

Project #7: Decoupage It!

The How-To

It's simple, really. Start by cutting out your images. If you are using intricate or small images, a little pair of nail scissors would be super helpful.

Clean the surface you're going to decoupage. If it needs painting first, make sure the paint is completely dry before you start, to avoid smudging.

Glue your pieces onto the surface, face up, with Mod-Podge or some other decoupage glue. Apply the glue to the surface and then stick your items down. Position your paper with your fingers. Wipe off any excess glue with a slightly damp sponge.

When you're all done, paint over the images with a clear, water-based varnish to seal everything and protect your piece from fingerprints, water, and the like. Many serious decoupagers recommend layering on, like, six or eight coats. You can, but I cheat. I do two. I've even just done—eek—one! Will my projects last forever and a day? Probably not. But they look awful perty right now.

●　●　●　●

Project #8: Sitting Pretty

Sure, your friends can sit on the floor, but wouldn't it be nice to offer them up a chair to sit on when they come over? Sure would. Read on.

Reupholster a beaten-down chair in a flash!

Cool chairs are a dime a dozen; the problem is that most of them are hiding out in some truly ugly outfits. To revive them and bring them back into the fray of cool, you just need a bit of glue and some fabric.

Choose a basic spray-on adhesive for regular fabrics and something like Liquid Nails for heavier fabrics such as vinyl or leather.

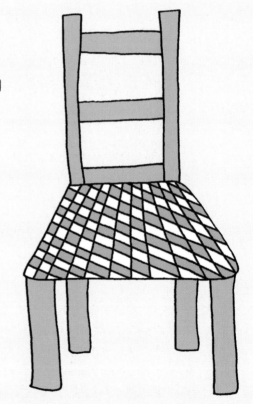

As for the fabric itself, buy a little more than it appears you need, for folding and such. But with most chairs, that's still not a lot of fabric, so look for remnants and scraps of lovely, once-expensive fabrics that are now marked down for quick sale.

What You Need

- Glue of choice
- Fabric
- Rubber gloves
- Scissors
- Heavy books
- Extra batting
- Screwdriver
- An old wooden chair in need of resuscitation (choose something that isn't wildly complicated, no easy chairs or the like—those need slipcovers, which are doable, but not with glue)

The HOW-TO

Remove the seat back and/or seat with a screwdriver. Remove the screws and pop the seat off. Cut your fabric to fit over the seat, leaving a good 6 inches of extra fabric all the way around.

Now take your stuff outside. This glue is mildly toxic. Actually, never spray any kind of glue or paint indoors if you can help it—it stinks!

Don your groovy rubber gloves and spray the back side of your fabric with a light coat of adhesive (if you spray too much, you run the risk of it bleeding through the fabric and leaving unsightly stains). Then proceed to wrap the seat like a present, making folds on the underside of the seat and spritzing a little more glue when you need to get a fold to stick. Make sure you flatten out any wrinkles by running your gloved hands over the fabric before it begins to set (which is right quick, so get to it!). Trim any excess fabric with your scissors. Place heavy books on top to add some pressure and help the gluing process along. Repeat with the seat back, and you're done. Let the glue dry thoroughly before reattaching the seat and seat back to the chair.

If your first chair-recovery job doesn't come out perfect, no problem. Just toss a pillow or throw blanket over the chair, and it will look casual and cool.

●   ●   ●   ●

Project #9:
Wacky Wicker

You know what I see at the local Salvation Army all the time?
Wicker. And honestly, in the past, I haven't been that jazzed
by it. I would walk on by, not really giving it a second look.
And then it popped into my head, a vision of beauty: a hot pink
wicker rocker! My mind was all a swirl, and I had to have that
rocker . . . and the wicker nightstand . . . and the wicker stool
. . . and the wicker dresser . . . and, well, you get the idea.

What You Need

- Something wicker
- Vibrant and bright spray paint
- Lots of newspaper

The HOW-TO

This one's so easy. You go outside. You spread out the newspaper. You plop the wicker piece in the center of the paper. You don trashy clothes. And you spray. Keep the spray can moving, and hold it five to seven inches away from the wicker. (And your face— fumes!) Keep a good distance from the wicker so the paint doesn't goop and glob and drip. Let dry and repeat.

Wicker is tricky to paint, thanks to all those little nooks and crannies, but it's worth it. People will gasp with shock and delight when they see your screaming orange wicker chair or your blinding yellow wicker chest! Oh, and don't hesitate to throw a terrifically bright and vivid pillow onto said chair or chest or stool.

Yowsa!

* * * *

Project #10:
A Chaise Lounge by Way of the Beach

You'd like a place to lounge about and read a book or talk on the phone, but those fancy upholstered chaises cost more than a sofa! What's a girl to do?

Um, make one—out of a beach chair!

Basically, you take a folding beach lounge chair—the kind you can find at any drugstore or superstore for around ten bucks—and you make a slipcover for it, hiding all the plastic webbing that makes the chair's unattractive yet undeniably comfortable seat.

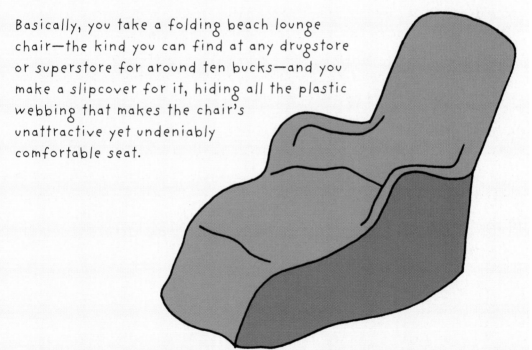

What You Need

- A folding beach lounge chair
- 3 yards of fabric (45 inches wide, which is standard)
- Scissors
- Pins
- Needle and thread or an iron and a roll of fusible web tape

The How-To

Unfold the chair and position it at your desired angle. Drape the 3 yards of fabric, with the right side of the fabric facing down, over the chair so that it falls to the floor over the back of the seat and also reaches the floor at the foot end. Center it so that you get an even drape on each side of the chair as well.

start with a folding beach lounge chair

Take your scissors and, starting on one side at the back leg, cut from the floor to the chair's seat, about 10 inches. Repeat on the other side.

Starting on one side of the chair, pin along the edge of the chair's back, all the way down to the seat. Repeat on the other side. Slip off the fabric and lay it out flat on an ironing board or on your floor.

If you want to stitch it up with needle and thread, use a straight stitch and follow along the line you created with the pins.

drape the fabric over the chair

If you are using the iron and fusible web tape, pull back the fabric gently to reveal the "seam" the pins have made. Remove one side of the fusible web tape, place the sticky side down along that pin line, and press down. Remove the second layer of paper from the fusible web tape and carefully press the fabric back together, smoothing out any wrinkles. Remove the pins and then iron. Repeat on the other side.

With either technique, once you've stitched or fused your seams together, carefully turn the slipcover right side out. Take your time and don't pull too hard. Slip this part over the back of the chair and drape the remaining length of fabric over the rest of the chair, allowing the fabric to hang over the sides and foot end.

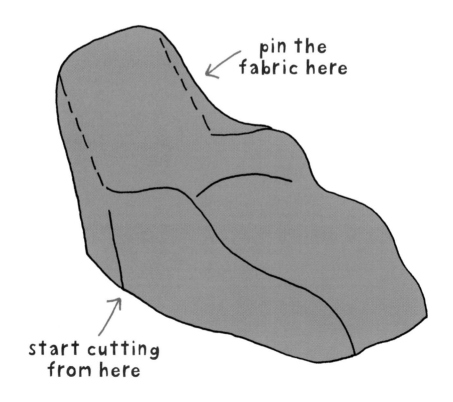

pin the
fabric here

start cutting
from here

Assess your chaise. If you like the looks of it, leave it as is. If, on the other hand, there are rough edges, from the fabric store cut or from your side cuts, hem the cut seams up with a straight stitch or some more fusible web and an iron.

Toss a throw pillow or two onto your new chaise, grab a good book, and kick back.

Alternate Idea: You could go a step further and pick up a "twin-size" package of batting. Why? Well, if you wrap the beach chair in the batting before you cover the chair, the end result will not look like a beach chair at all! It will in fact look like a plump, cushy chaise lounge, the kind elegant women lay upon while eating bonbons. Simply lay the batting on the whole chair and secure with a little spray adhesive underneath (do this outside) or even some masking tape (tape the batting on the underside, as if you were wrapping a present). Then proceed with the "upholstering" instructions above.

•   •   •   •

CHAPTER SIX
organize and focus

. . . .

What's left? Golly, where do you put your CDs? Your dirty clothes?
What about study supplies? And your makeup? This chapter is all
about the little things that make your room function well while it's
looking pretty.

. . . .

Project #1: Suitcase Storage

Suitcases make great storage. You can put your CDs inside. You can
put your bikinis in one in the winter and then use it again in the
summer to store sweaters. You can store stationary in 'em. Books.
Letters from days
gone by. Your diaries
from the last three
years (some have
locks and keys!).
Jewelry. Craft
supplies. Your
Barbie collection
that you don't
want your
friends to know
about. Anything.

But where can you find such suitcases, and will they be cute? The answer, dear friend, is at the local thrift. Vintage suitcases—the hard kind—are supremely cool, no matter what they're made of. They just need a little cleaning before you put them to use. And maybe some "cute-ifying."

When shopping for suitcases, look for the aforementioned hard-sided variety. Make sure the click-clicks work—you know, the latches at the top—and that the handle isn't broken. You should be able to find some fairly effortlessly for just a few bucks in no time. Bring them home and open them up outside, airing their old stories and smells for the whole world to enjoy. Spray the suitcases down with some disinfectant spray like Lysol, then maybe even a fabric cleanser. Let them air out for days like this so they have time to dry.

As for the outside of the case, if it's plastic, don a pair of yellow plastic gloves. Nab a bucket, a bottle of bleach, and the hose. Mix one part bleach to four parts water and scrub the outside of the suitcase, ridding it of its years of grime. If your case is wood or cardboard, you'll need a gentle furniture cleanser and a dry cloth. If your case is metal, go for window cleanser and a nice soft dishtowel.

If your suitcase is wood, cardboard, or metal, it probably has a nice patina (that's an "old glow") about it, and it's best to clean it, then leave it as is. If your suitcase is plastic, you have the option of changing the color and painting it up all pretty. But think about it first: Is this funky avocado green actually cool? Will it look neat and keen in your pink bedroom? My answer is a hearty "Yes!" But if the answer for you is "No!" read on.

What You Need

- Acrylic paint in two or more colors

- Paintbrush

- A piece of cardboard or a sheet of acetate (for the stencil)

- Spray paint sealer

- Masking tape

- A hard-sided suitcase

The How-To

Once the suitcase is clean and dry, use tape to cover any parts you don't want to paint, like the latches or possibly the handle. Lay out a lot of newspaper outside and put the suitcase down on the paper. Brush a solid but thin coat of paint over the entire suitcase. Let it dry overnight. Paint on a second layer of the same color and let it dry for another night.

Cut out a stencil—it could be a simple circle or a star or birds. (Find an image, print it off your computer or blow it up at the copy shop, and then cut it out, leaving behind a stencil.) Put the stencil down on the suitcase and paint the second color over the stencil, making sure not to paint outside the stencil sheet. Remove the stencil, wipe it off, and place it down again somewhere else on the case, adding more circles or stars or birds. Let it dry.

When the whole case is dry, you'll want to spray on the sealer. Make sure you do this outside in a well-ventilated area (and please, not near any open windows!). You should even tie a scarf around your mouth and nose to protect yourself from flying harmful chemicals. This stuff is toxic.

Let the sealer dry and then do it again, adding a second protective coating. Once the case is **finally** dry, bring it inside and store your stuff!

● ● ● ●

Photo-Adorned Boxes

I throw a lot of my craft stuff, jewelry, makeup, and more into old shoe boxes that I've covered with decoupage or even fabric and a little glue. But how do I tell one from the next? Easy. I take a digital picture of what is inside, then I paste or tape it to the front of the box. Then I know what is inside of each box AND my boxes look supercool.

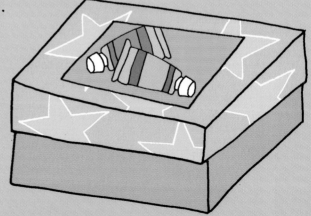

Project #2:
Hot Hot Hangers

Wood hangers can cost a lot of money, but I'm here to tell you, look around the variety-type shops like Kmart and Target, and you'll find a bulk deal. Wood hangers are so much nicer to your clothes than wire or plastic hangers. And after you've painted them up all pretty, they are such works of art, you could even give them as gifts.

What You Need

- Several wood hangers

- Paint and brush (or spray paint will work too)

- Paper images small enough to fit onto the solid part of the hanger

- Masking tape

- Ribbon

- Clear decoupage glue

The HOW-TO

Cut your images out with small scissors and set them aside.

Put some newspaper down on the ground outside. Lay the hangers out on the paper. If you're spray painting, cover the metal tops of the hangers with the tape. Paint the hangers. While the paint is still a bit wet, arrange your cutout images on the hangers and let 'em dry in place.

Once the hangers are dry, seal your images with Mod-Podge or clear glue. Tie a 6- to 8-inch piece of ribbon into a bow at the base of each metal hook.

Not only will your hangers look pretty, but because you're using wood hangers now, your clothing will stretch out less and quite possibly last longer. And this is a great gift for almost anyone (everyone has clothes; everyone needs hangers!). Wrap up a set of three in a little tissue paper and present them to your mom, sister, or best friend.

● ● ● ●

Project #3:
Really Weird but Wacky Hamper

Need a place to put your dirty clothes? How about an old man's shirt? Weird? Yes. Useful? **Yes!**

What You Need

- A large man's dress shirt

- A hanger (one of your painted wooden ones would be nice)

- Needle and thread

The HOW-TO

Turn the shirt inside out. If the shirt has a curved bottom hem, cut across the hem to make it straight. Cut off the sleeves. With your needle and thread and a backstitch, sew the armholes up and then sew the bottom seams together, sealing it up. Essentially, you're turning the shirt into a bag, and the bottom of the shirt is the bottom of the bag.

Now turn the shirt/bag right side out and put it on your hanger as if it were still a shirt. Unbutton the top button or two to provide a large enough hole to slide your dirties through. Hang this on a hook, hang the hook on the door to your closet, and toss your first smelly sock into the neck. When your new bag is full, cart it off to the washing machine. And, hey, if the bag itself gets stinky, just toss it in the washer too!

Alternate Idea: Don't feel like sewing today? You can do this in about a minute if you just nab a rubber band. Don't cut the arms of the shirt off. Turn the shirt inside out, bunch up the bottom in your hand and secure it with a rubber band as if it were a ponytail. Make sure the rubber band is **really** tightly wound. Turn the shirt right side out, and hang it up. The arms may dangle freely at the sides, but projects don't get any easier than this.

• • • •

Paint cans

Paint cans make the cutest little buckets for your makeup, pens, pencils, art supplies, and more. But they are always so dirty, still filled with crusty leftover paint! Why not pick up brand-spanking-new ones? Big hardware stores usually have both quart-size and gallon-size empty metal paint cans for sale. They have never been used—and are therefore bright, shiny, and clean! And cheap, too; the quart size usually costs around a buck. You can leave them as is or decoupage them till the cows come home. They would even make great gift boxes. Remember this when your best pal's birthday rolls around!

Project #4:
Lap Desk

You want to study in bed, but you don't have anything to write on, other than one of the heavy volumes of the **World Book** perched on your knees. Ow.

Be nice to that lap.
Make a lap desk!

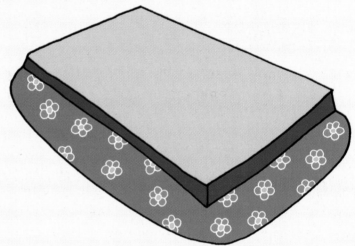

What You Need

- A pillow—a flatter one, as opposed to poofy, is best

- A cute pillowcase

- Velcro

- Glue

- Needle and thread

- A piece of scrap wood, a quarter inch thick or *less*, cut to the size of the pillow (ask your friendly handyman at the local hardware store to cut it to your measurements; most will do it for free!)

- Sandpaper

- Spray-on varnish

The HOW-To

Sew a strip of Velcro to the open end of your pillowcase, fuzzy side to one inner opening, rough side to the other, so that you can close up the pillowcase with a Velcro seal.

Take the piece of wood outside. Sand the edges of the wood down so they are no longer sharp or pointy. Spread out a lot of newspaper. Spray a thin layer of varnish over the wood. Let it dry and then repeat. You could stain the wood first, maybe to match your bedroom furniture. Or you could paint the wood a color or even decoupage photos to it. Still, you should varnish it when you're done decorating it.

Once it's completely dry, glue down four fuzzy strips of Velcro all the way around, about 3 inches from the edge of the wood. Then sew or glue the "male" part of the Velcro to the pillowcase, so that the two line up.

Stick the desk part to the pillow part and kick back in bed with your newly constructed lap desk on your very own lap! You can remove the pillow part and even the pillowcase when it comes time to wash it. In time the pillow will form to your legs a bit, and it will be **très** comfortable!

Project #5: Wall Organizer

This is perfect for over your desk or next to a bulletin board or chalkboard. But it can also go next to your mirror or above a vanity, and instead of holding pens and scissors, it could hold makeup and jewelry.

What You Need

- A piece of sturdy fabric, approximately 16 x 20 inches (I like wool felt best because it doesn't have to be hemmed, but certainly upholstery fabric or backcloth would work too.)

- Another piece of fabric, about the same size, in a coordinating color

- Needle and thread (even embroidery thread would work)

- Two pushpins

The HOW-TO

Lay the first piece of fabric out flat. Assess the items you want to put in pockets, then cut pocket shapes accordingly from the second piece of fabric. For instance, you could make a pocket about 8 x 4 inches for your scissors and another that is 6 x 4 inches, just the right size for your hole punch. The same-size pocket would work for a hairbrush if you're creating this for your dressing area. For pencils, cut a pocket 4 x 10 inches. We'll sew mini pockets within your organizer in a moment.

Arrange the pocket shapes on the flat piece of fabric so that they fit nicely and aren't crowding one another. With your needle and thread, sew down the pockets on three sides, leaving the top of each pocket open. Do this with a simple straight stitch. For the 4 x 10 pencil pocket, first sew up all three sides, then go back and sew vertical lines from the top of the pocket to the bottom, 1½–2 inches apart.

Add your goods—school supplies or beauty supplies—and pin your new organizer to the wall with two pushpins.

●　●　●　●

Project #6:
Light-Switch covers

I started making these many, many years ago. After I'd made one for my room, I started making them for the whole house! They also make great personalized gifts for friends; just use pictures or magazine cutouts that are meaningful to them.

What You Need

- A cheap, plain, plastic light-switch cover (to remove your existing one and use that, turn off the light and nab a screwdriver; undo two little screws, and—pop!—it comes off)

- A picture from a magazine you like or a scrap of wallpaper or a scrap of fantastic wrapping paper

- Masking tape

- Scissors

The HOW-TO

Place the switch plate on the paper you've chosen, both items facedown. Center the plate on the design as you like. Note that if it's a picture of a person, you will be cutting out a hole in the center for the switch part, so plan accordingly.

With a pencil, outline the switch-plate cover. Make another rough outline, about an inch from the outer edges, all the way around the plate. Then lightly run your pencil around the inside of the switch rectangle, marking it for cutting. Cut out the shape of the switch-plate cover using the outermost pencil marks as your guide. But do not cut the small rectangle out! Instead, with a small pair of scissors, cut an X across the entire small rectangle.

Place the image over the switch-plate cover now, aligning the X over the switch hole. Fold each small triangle from the X through the hole and secure them onto the back with a piece of tape. Smooth out the rest of the image across the cover, folding the edges around to the back of the cover and securing them with more masking tape.

Poke your two screws from behind to make holes in the front for the screws and then screw the plate back in place.

Now you'll smile every time you turn your light on or off!

A Touch of Nature

Have you ever seen an air plant? I grew up in Florida,
where every truck stop was selling mini air plants, but
perhaps you have never seen these living works of art.
Air plants do not grow in the ground. They don't really
grow in the air, but they sort of look like they do; they
grow on branches or rocks. All their moisture is absorbed
through their leaves, which are covered in scales called
"trichomes."

They make great living art,
terrific room décor. You can
hang them on a wall or
from a ceiling or off the
corner of your bed.
Otherwise known
as "tillandsia,"
they bloom when
they are mature
and then spawn
little baby plants off their
base. Air plants have a
decidedly sinister look
to them, all points and
angles. They are often gray
or icy green in color, but
they come in oranges and
reds, too, and often have

pink or purple flowers.
They can last for
years and
years on
a little bit
of natural
light and some
infrequent watering.
But how do you water
a plant with no pot? A spray mister! (No tap water,
though; it must be distilled water, which is available at
any grocery store.) And they love humidity, so go ahead
and bring an air plant into the bathroom with you when
you take your shower. All in all, these wild and wacky
plants are so much cooler than your average variety.

the outro

. . . .

Oh Lovely Reader, My Interior Decorating Diva Pal,

The whole goal of these **I Wanna**...books is to inspire you and give you a skeleton of knowledge that you can take back with you to your room, where you can dream, create, make, build, paint, and craft your very own new things. Making stuff for yourself and others is a worthwhile activity and gosh-darn fun, too. It allows you to indulge the artistic impulses you have swirling about in your brain. Good crafting = love!

The next book in the series will hopefully inspire you to create lovely and wondrous presents for everyone on your gift list. You will be filled to the brim with home-cooked ideas, instructions on how to make glorious gifts that will make all your pals feel way special.

I had a blast making this stuff with you all in mind. Share the love, keep spreading the crafty gospel, and get your hands dirty for me!

Rock on, clea